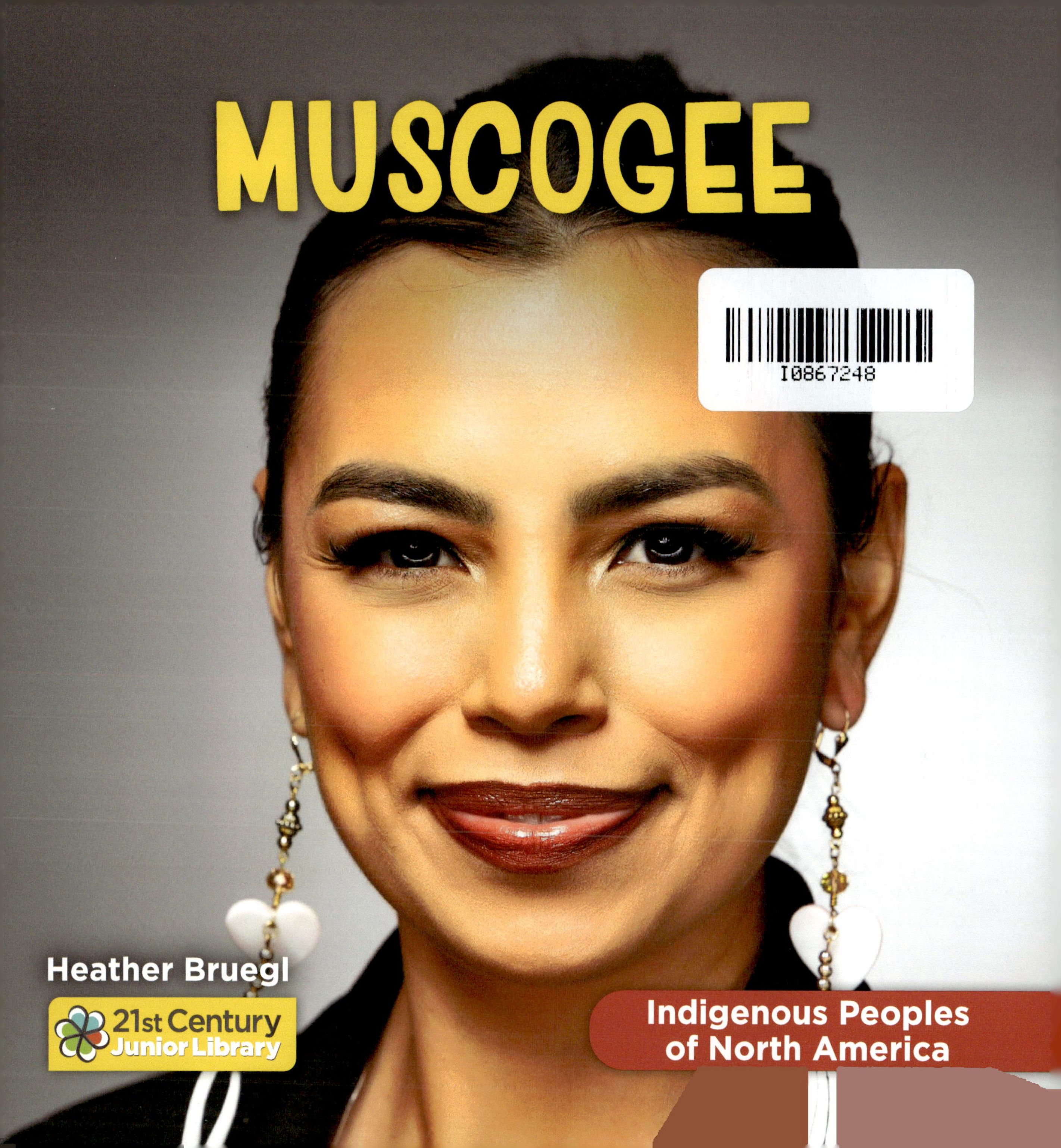

MUSCOGEE

Heather Bruegl

21st Century Junior Library

Indigenous Peoples of North America

Published in the United States of America by:

Cherry Lake Press
2395 South Huron Parkway, Suite 200, Ann Arbor, Michigan 48104
www.cherrylakepress.com

Reading Adviser: Beth Walker Gambro, MS, Ed., Reading Consultant, Yorkville, IL
Content Advisers: Department of Culture and Humanities and the Historic and Cultural Preservation Department, Muscogee (Creek) Nation

Photo Credits: © Isabel Coronado, cover, title page; © Muscogee Nation Office of Public Relations, 5, 19; © RaeLynn Butler, 6; © Jay Reeves/ASSOCIATED PRESS, 9; © Denice Dotson, 10 (left); © Sthanlee B. Mirador/Sipa USA via AP, 10 (right); © Midge Dellinger, 11; © Ryon M/Shutterstock, 12; © Field Museum via Muscogee (Creek) Nation, 15; © Sarah J Malerich/Wikimedia Commons via CC BY-SA 3.0, 17; © Vasha Hunt/ASSOCIATED PRESS, 20; © Michael Warren/ASSOCIATED PRESS, 21

Cherry Lake Press is an imprint of Cherry Lake Publishing Group.

Library of Congress Cataloging-in-Publication Data has been filed and is available at catalog.loc.gov

Cherry Lake Publishing Group would like to acknowledge the work of the Partnership for 21st Century Learning, a Network of Battelle for Kids. Please visit Battelle for Kids online for more information.

Printed in the United States of America

Note from publisher: Websites change regularly, and their future contents are outside of our control. Supervise children when conducting any recommended online searches for extended learning opportunities.

About the Content Advisers: Grateful acknowledgment is given to the staff of the Department of Culture and Humanities and the Historic and Cultural Preservation Department of the Muscogee (Creek) Nation, without whom this book would not have been possible. These departments ensure the protection and preservation of valued historic and cultural resources for future generations. The Muscogee (Creek) Nation National Library and Archives digital resources include original documents, photos, recorded interviews, and a Mvskoke language dictionary for all who wish to learn more about Mvskoke people and their history.

About the Cover: Isabel Coronado is a citizen of Muscogee (Creek) Nation and policy expert working to bring awareness and solutions to issues facing children of incarcerated parents. She's a fierce advocate for community, state, and federal policies that keep families together and that help children grow and flourish in supportive environments.

Cherry Lake Press

CONTENTS

WHO WE ARE

The ancestors of the Muscogee (Creek) people lived in the southeastern United States for thousands of years. The people call themselves Mvskoke (mus-KOH-kee). "Mvskoke" is the correct spelling using the Mvskoke Nation's alphabet. The word "Creek" came from British **colonizers** because Mvskoke towns were near rivers.

Think!

RaeLynn Butler is the Muscogee (Creek) Nation Secretary of Culture and Humanities. She helps protect and share Mvskoke and Euchee language, culture, history, arts, and cultural resources. Why do you think this is an important job?

The Mvskoke are **descendants** of the Mississippian Culture. They built impressive towns and earthen mounds used for ceremonies and important gatherings. Some of these mounds remain today. They are **sacred** to the Mvskoke people. Mvskoke tribal towns and clans have always been central to Mvskoke identity.

Members of the Arbeka Ceremonial Ground tribal town gather at Choccolocco Park in Oxford, Alabama.

Make a Guess!

The Muscogee did not have a written language for much of their history. How do you think they passed down their history and knowledge? Research to find out if you are right.

Many southeastern tribes formed the Mvskoke **Confederacy**, a powerful alliance founded on shared culture and protection. The Euchee people, who speak a distinct language, have lived alongside the Mvskoke for generations, and remain a part of the Muscogee (Creek) Nation today.

Mvskoke people believe in a Creator who makes all living things. Plants, animals, humans, water, and the land are all connected. This belief is part of the Mvskoke culture and worldview.

OUR LIVES TODAY

Today, most Mvskoke live on the Muscogee (Creek) Reservation located in northeastern Oklahoma. The Mvskoke Nation has more than 100,000 citizens, making it one of the largest **federally recognized** tribal nations in the United States. Its capital is Okmulgee, which means "bubbling water."

Mvskoke people live around the world. Some serve in the U.S. military. Others are doctors, teachers, artists, police officers, and musicians. Mvskoke citizens work in nearly every profession.

U.S. Air Force veteran Butch McIntosh and retired U.S. Marine Curtis Smith lead the Muscogee (Creek) Nation Honor Guard at a Mvskoke celebration in Oxford, Alabama.

Joy Harjo is a world-famous Mvskoke poet. She served as the U.S. **Poet Laureate** from 2019 to 2022. She was the first Indigenous poet to do so.

Sterlin Harjo is a Mvskoke citizen who has produced and directed numerous films and television shows, including the critically acclaimed TV series *Reservation Dogs*.

Joy Harjo

Create!

Find and read Joy Harjo's poem "Remember." Write your own poem in a similar style about what you think is important to remember.

Sterlin Harjo

Midge Dellinger

Midge Dellinger is a Mvskoke citizen and oral historian for the Mvskoke Nation. She records Mvskoke people sharing stories and oral traditions, making sure that Mvskoke culture, language, and history are passed on to younger generations.

Talladega National Forest in Alabama lies within Mvskoke traditional territory.

OUR ANCESTRAL LANDS

To the Mvskoke people, the land is sacred. Their **ancestral** homelands covered what are now the states of Georgia, Alabama, Florida, Tennessee, North Carolina, South Carolina, and Mississippi. Mvskoke families planted crops, such as the **Three Sisters**. They gathered fruits, nuts, and medicinal plants. They hunted and fished through the changing seasons, taking only what they needed and always using every part of the animal or plant.

As European settlers moved into the Southeast, the Mvskoke Confederacy disagreed on how to respond. The Mvskoke way of life began to change. Some wanted to trade and work with settlers. Others believed it was too dangerous. These disagreements led to a civil war within the Mvskoke Confederacy.

Eventually, U.S. policies, like the 1830 Indian Removal Act, forced the Mvskoke to give up their homelands. More than 23,000 people had to leave.

Look!

Look at the removal map on page 15. What do you notice?

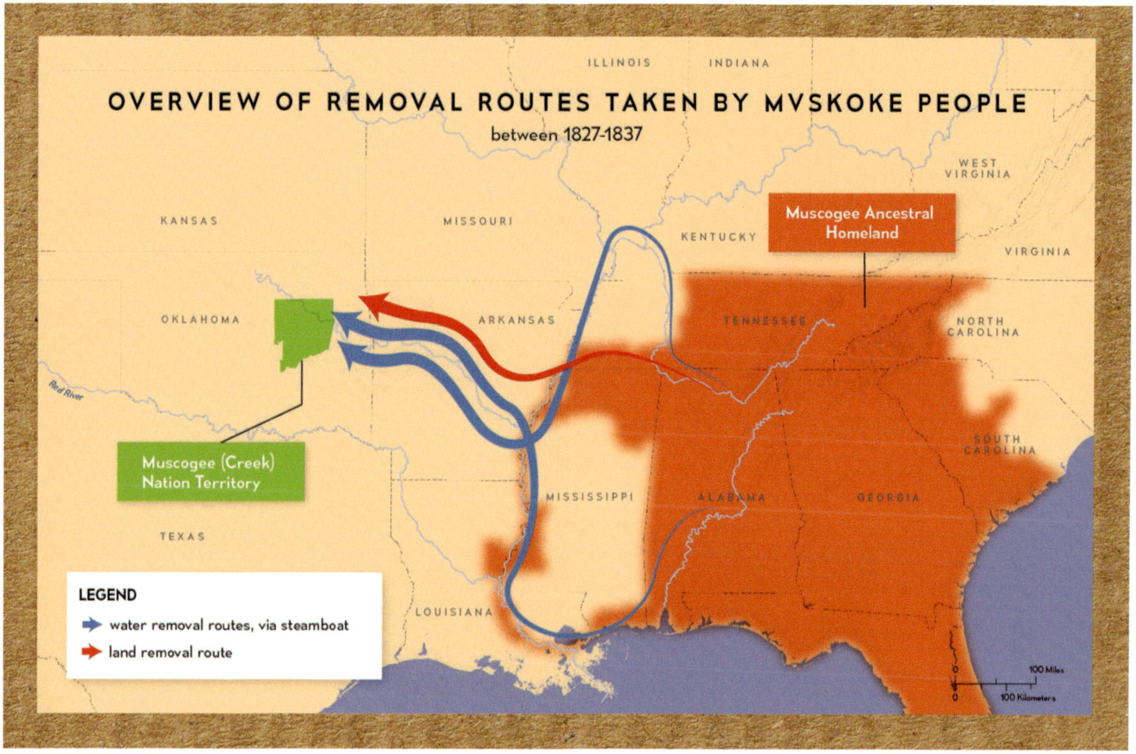

U.S. soldiers rounded up families with only what they could carry. Most walked more than 750 miles to Indian Territory, now present-day Oklahoma. Others traveled by steamboat. Around 4,000 people died during their journey.

The Mvskoke Nation survived this tragic event. The Mvskoke people rebuilt their communities and continued their traditions, honoring the strength and **resilience** of their ancestors.

Ask Questions!

What questions do you have about the Mvskoke people's journey to rebuild their communities? Work with an adult to explore Muscogee (Creek) Nation National Library and Archives resources to find answers to your questions.

Mvskoke leaders carried the ashes of their ceremonial fires to relight them in their new home. This memorial stands in honor of the fires that never went out.

CARRYING TRADITIONS FORWARD

Today, the Mvskoke people continue to practice their culture and traditions. Together, the Mvskoke people work to help maintain strong community ties and connect younger generations to their heritage. The Mvskoke and Euchee Language Programs teach these languages in schools, community classes, and homes to keep them alive.

Every summer, the Mvskoke Nation hosts the Mvskoke Festival, a celebration held for over 50 years. Families and friends gather to dance, play traditional games, watch a rodeo, enjoy concerts, share food, cheer at sports events, and ride carnival rides. It is a joyful time to celebrate being Mvskoke.

Muscogee (Creek) Nation historic Council House serves as a museum and cultural center.

The Mvskoke Nation also keeps its connection to ancestral lands. Hickory Ground (Oce Vpofv), the last Mvskoke capital in the Southeast, remains a sacred place in Alabama. In Georgia, the Mvskoke Nation helps to protect the Ocmulgee Mounds National Historical Park.

George Thompson, Mekko, and Robin Soweka, Traditional Cultural Advisor, speak at Hickory Ground in Alabama.

Tracie Revis is a Mvskoke and Yuchi citizen who works to share the importance of the Ocmulgee Mounds in Georgia.

Each year, during the Ocmulgee Mounds Indigenous Celebration, Mvskoke people return to honor their ancestors and traditions.

Today, the Muscogee (Creek) Nation remains a **sovereign** nation and continues to build a strong future for Mvskoke people.

GLOSSARY

ancestral (an-SEH-struhl) belonging to past generations of a family or cultural group

colonizers (KAH-luh-nie-zerz) people who settle in an area under the leadership of a government and exercise control over Indigenous peoples

confederacy (kuhn-FEH-duh-ruh-see) a group of people or nations joined for a common purpose

descendants (dih-SEN-duhnts) people who come from a certain ancestor or ancestors

federally recognized (FEH-duh-ruh-lee REH-kig-niezd) a status assigned to U.S. tribal nations by the federal government that provides specific rights and benefits

mekko (MEE-koh) a Mvskoke tribal town chief

poet laureate (POH-uht LOR-ee-uht) a poet honored by a country's government for achievement

resilience (rih-ZIL-yuhns) the ability and strength to make it through and rebuild after tragedy or extreme hardship

sacred (SAY-kruhd) holy; important to a system of belief

sovereign (SAH-vruhn) independent; having the right to govern oneself

Three Sisters (THREE SIH-sterz) a form of planting in Indigenous communities involving corn, beans, and squash

FIND OUT MORE

Books

Bruegl, Heather. *Indigenous Peoples and Military Service.* Ann Arbor, MI: Cherry Lake Publishing, 2024.

Sorell, Traci. *We Are Still Here! Native American Truths Everyone Should Know.* Watertown, MA: Charlesbridge, 2021.

Online

With an adult, explore more online with these suggested searches.

- Muscogee (Creek) Nation National Library and Archives
- Ocmulgee Mounds National Historical Park, National Park Service

Say Hello!

Hesci (HEES-chay) is a way to say "hello" in the Muscogee language.

INDEX

ABOUT THE AUTHOR

Heather Bruegl, a member of the Oneida Nation of Wisconsin/Stockbridge-Munsee, is a Madonna University graduate with a Master of Arts in U.S. History. She is a public historian and decolonial educator, and her Munsee name is Kiishookunkwe, meaning "Sunflower in Full Bloom." Heather frequently travels to present on Indigenous history, policy, and activism, bringing her deep knowledge and personal connection to the subject.